The Book of Staff Spinning

COMPILED, WRITTEN AND ILLUSTRATED BY

JOHNATHAN REYNOLDS

The Book of Staff Spinning

Published by Butterfingers Books, England.

www.butterfingersbooks.co.uk

Cover design by Ricardo Pereira Campos.

Illustrations and type setting by Johnathan Reynolds.

Printed by Scotprint.

A C.I.P. Catalogue record for this title is available from the British Library.

ISBN: 978-1-898591-20-7

www.homeofstaff.com

Introduction

Welcome to Staff Spinning!

Staff spinning is a hypnotic and highly visual performance art which creates circular patterns all around you. It is appropriate to mention that the staff has been a weapon in various martial art disciplines for thousands of years; this is its origin. However, in this book I will be focusing on the performance art side of staff, that said if you're looking for martial arts then this is not the book for you.

The staff is really just a long stick, often decorated, weighted on both ends or 'wicked' ready for fire spinning. It also has many other names from other places and cultures around the world, Bo staff, canes and sticks to name just a few.

Staffs have been around in one form or another evolving through time, use and culture. Many of the great moves and a good deal of techniques were created and evolved from a few martial art forms such as Eskrima and Aikido, which both use Bo and Jo staffs; other cultures like the Polynesian Fire Dancers use short fire staffs in dance. The Indian Silambam staff has been used as a weapon since at least the 2nd century, evident from references in ancient Sangam literature of the time.

Due to the sheer number of staff moves that exist, this book is designed to teach you the core movements and principles needed to understand staff spinning and take it to the next level. From these moves, you will be able to understand how to invent your own tricks and develop your own style.

If you are completely new to 'spinning' and would call yourself a beginner, just keep reading! The basics section (see page 14) will show you everything you need to know to start spinning. By the end of the basics section you should be looking good and feeling like you are a true staff spinner.

If this isn't the first time you've played with a staff and you feel like you know a bit already you may want to skip ahead to the "Intermediate" and "Advanced" sections, where you will find an assortment of new tricks that will push you as far as you want to go. It's always worth remembering to skim the basics section first to be sure you are ready.

Staff spinning has a steep learning curve at the beginning, but not to worry, within a few weeks you will be feeling the momentum of staff spinning and impressing your friends. I should warn you now, expect a few bruises and bumps at the beginning, but soon you will be spinning rotors and throwing tricks! (See disclaimer page 2). Some tricks will take longer to learn than others, so take your time and if you get stuck, take a break. Some tricks like the behind the back moves require a certain amount of flexibility to do. I would suggest warming up, followed by a few upper body stretches to loosen you up a bit and increase your range of motion before starting. This is really important as you can hurt yourself if you are not warmed up properly.

JOHNATHAN REYNOLDS

Brighton, May 2009

Acknowledgements

There are just so many people to thank that helped me in the creation of this book.

To all of you who helped me over the years by teaching me tricks, concepts and showing me the ropes, I implore you to continue the way of sharing and teaching that made me who I am now. I can only hope that in writing this book I in some small way have given that gift back to the spinning community, just as you have given to me.

My greatest of thanks go to the special people in my life who directly helped me in putting this book together.

In particular:

My amazing wife and partner in life, Helen Reynolds, who guided me in so many ways, gave me the space I needed to work, and always made sure I was as happy as I could be.

Bill Harder, my Grandfather who showed me the martial art way when I was young and gave me the seed of determination to do something I always enjoy .

Dev Kev who is a great spinning mentor to me, who helped greatly in checking that this book is technically correct and gave many useful ideas and insights from his years of experience.

Adrian Nerra who helped make this book so much smoother to read.

Loz Egginton for providing so much help with many ideas for the book including a lot of the choreographic concepts and suggestions.

Marion and Roger Prentice who proof read this book and made it more readable.

Laurie Collard of Butterfingers Books for having the faith to publish this.

Thank you so much!

Contents

How To Use This Book

This book has been designed for you to easily find and perform any trick you want to try, but it is essential to master the basics before you try the more advanced stuff. To learn moves, it helps to identify the difference between the two ends of the staff i.e. which end is "leading". Some people tie coloured fabric to the ends of the staff to help see what is going on during the learning phases.

In this book you will be able to see which end is top because it is marked with a light grey direction arrow, while the bottom is a black direction arrow. The top end (End A, also known as the leader end) of the staff is also the end that is closest to your thumb when holding the staff with one hand. End B or the bottom of the staff is closest to the little finger (pinky finger). Please see illustrations on the KEY page to the right for examples of this.

Don't think about it too much when you get stuck on a move, it is often much harder to understand than to do. Take a break and come back to it later with a clear mind. Often it just "clicks" all of a sudden when you least expect it.

It is also worth mentioning that this book is only a reference to some of the more popular moves and tricks at this time. There are way too many out there to try and put all of them in a book, but there is enough here to get you started.

Keep in mind that many tricks have many different names - don't worry about the 'right' name too much, just focus on what the move involves. Every teacher has a different way of explaining and naming things, so I have used the names which are most obvious to me.

All tricks are cross-referenced in the book, letting you know if there are tricks you must master first to proceed. The advanced section contains the brain-freezing moves! It will give you ideas of where to go with your new knowledge and how to best use it. This is also where I show you the double staff stuff. If you don't like a trick or the trick doesn't suit your style, leave it and move on to something you find more interesting. It is all about enjoying yourself and having fun. If you feel like you have something new and incredible that needs to be included in the next version of The Book of Staff Spinning please let me know.

For other ideas and tips for what you can do with these moves, read the small print at the bottom of the pages.

KEY:

To help you while using the illustrations in this book, I have used an easy identification direction arrow system.

The staff's "top end" also known as "end **A**", or "thumb end" will use a light grey arrow.

The staff's "bottom end" also known as "end **B**", or "pinky end" will use a black arrow.

These arrows try to show the best view possible to demonstrate which way the staffs should be spinning.

Remember to look at the feet in the illustrations to figure out which way to be facing.

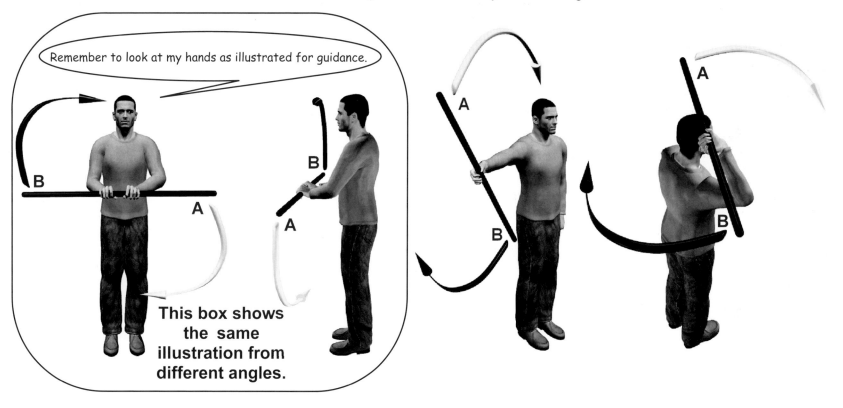

Remember to look at my hands as illustrated for guidance.

This box shows the same illustration from different angles.

Introducing... The Staff

A staff is just a stick that has a good weight, length and thickness for spinning. It will often have many different types of attachments on the ends of the stick. Here is a common staff used for what we want.

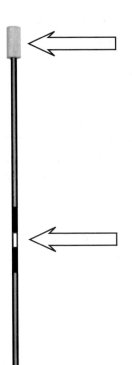

Most staffs have some kind of attachment on the end depending on the use of the staff. For training it is a good idea to attach tennis balls on the ends to soften the impact when you hit yourself. Another great attachment for training is coloured flags or ribbons. These will allow you to see the planes and movement of the staff during the learning curve. See page 86 for wicks.

The handle is there to help grip the staff while spinning. A commonly used grip is found on tennis rackets, but many other grips work well too. It will also help you feel where the centre of your staff is. Another great idea is to mark the centre of the staff with highly visible tape which will help you visually keep your centre while spinning.

The shaft can be made of many types of materials (e.g. Wood, metal, fibreglass etc. See the next page for more details on materials.) This allows the user to customise the right length, weight and thickness for best use of the staff.

Types of Staffs

There are different kinds of staffs out there. A few of the most common are:

Long staff

Short staff

Contact staff

Baton

Cane

Fire staff

Glow / UV / Light staff

S-Staff / Buugeng Staff

Martial Arts Staffs:

Quarter staff

Hanbo (3 foot),

Tanjo or Eskrima Staff (2 foot)

Jo staff (4 foot)

Bo or Rokushakubo staff (6 foot)

Selecting the Right Staff For You

Much like a snowboarder or skier will use different sized and weighted boards and skis a staff spinner must chose what is right for him/her.

For beginners I would recommend a stick about the height of your shoulder. The diameter of staff is a very personal choice for the spinner, with basic sizes normally ranging between 1.5 cm (a bit thicker than a pen) and 3.5 cm (about a shovel handle). Most professional staffs average about 2 cm, which for most people is a good comfortable size to begin with.

It is worth attaching foam to each end while learning as this will help soften the blow when you eventually hit yourself.

Also see www.homeofstaff.com for buying ready made fire staffs.

Staff Materials

The 2 main materials staffs are made from: Wood and Aluminium.

(For staff decorations see page 97)

Wooden poles are normally heavier then metal poles, but they are a cheap and easy staff to learn with. The weight will help the staff move slower which will help teach you good technique during learning. Wooden dowelling or a mop handle from a hardware store is perfect.

An aluminium staff is in my opinion by far the best material to use. It is light, very strong, fire proof, dissipates heat well, won't splinter, and is naturally shiny. The best source for aluminium poles will be your nearest plumbing or hardware store. Otherwise metal mop handle poles work well, as do shower rods.

Once you have outgrown your mop handle, you will probably want a staff made by professionals who make staffs for professional staff spinners. Check out the great range at www.homeofstaff.com.

Short Staff

The shorter the staff, the faster the circles and the tighter the spins.

Short staffs (e.g. batons) are much smaller, lighter and compact. This makes them easier to carry around and allows you to use tighter spaces to practice indoors. They are great for throwing and double staff techniques as they allow an extra set of moves that would not be possible with a long staff. When the staff length is slightly shorter than twice your arm length you can spin in some extra planes, as illustrated below.

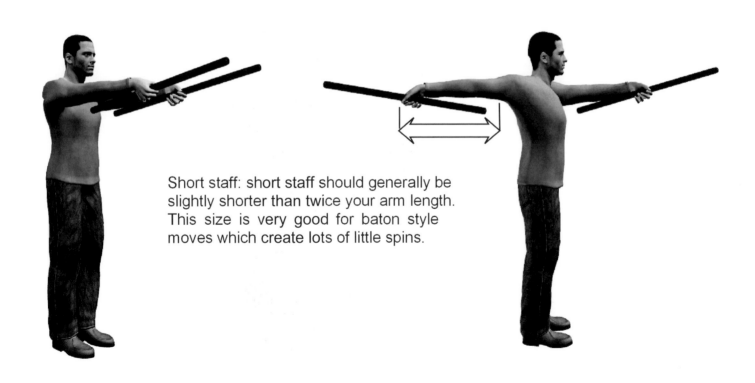

Short staff: short staff should generally be slightly shorter than twice your arm length. This size is very good for baton style moves which create lots of little spins.

Long Staff

While long staff moves are a lot slower due to the length and weight, the wide diameter of its spin makes it seem much more graceful. Even so, due to the heavier weight it can gather both speed and momentum which makes it a great choice for single staff spinning, isolation moves (see page 68) and contact moves (see page 51). However, a longer staff will mean you will need larger practice spaces, and it is easier to hurt yourself with a long staff as the weight and momentum is usually greater. Remember, it is a good idea not to have it much taller than your head, as this can limit the number of moves you can do, (see illustration below).

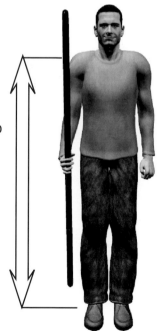

Floor to shoulder height is a good length to begin with as it gives the widest diameter of spin without constant danger of the staff hitting the ground.

The Theory

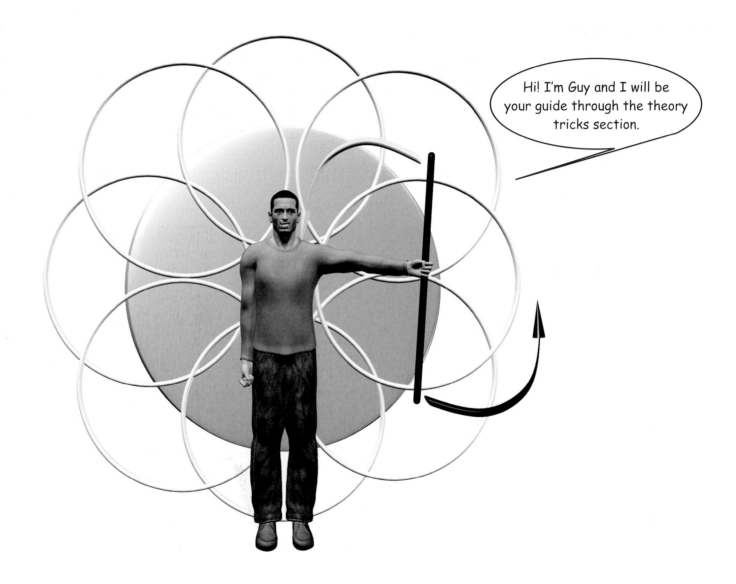

Holding the Staff

There are many holds used to keep the staff spinning. Until you are ready for the advanced moves like finger spins (see page 63) and palm spinning (see page 56), it is best to have a really secure hold on the staff. To do this, grasp the staff firmly with your hand, (see illustration 2) - this is called a full handed grip and it helps ensure that you don't drop it. It does not matter which hand you use as everything must be learned in both hands eventually, but most people like starting with their dominant hand. When using both hands make sure that your hands are always using the strongest grip possible, (see illustration 1).

There also comes a time when you know to relax your grip, allowing the staff to spin a little more freely in some moves. For now a good strong solid grip is needed.

1   2

Speed

Speed comes later... It is important to note that speed will come with practice, but first you must learn the technique. If you are having problems with a move, slow down. Only when you feel you have fixed the problem increase the speed. This way, when you wish to speed up, your arms will have acquired muscle memory.

Planes and Body Directions

Planes are invisible arcs or imaginary walls that travel directly through you in every direction. These planes use small circles, which should normally be made with / from the wrist (illustration 1). The arm moves in large circles, moving the spinning staff to different planes for different tricks (illustration 3). See the following pages for more on different planes. To make a trick smooth, make sure that the staff is travelling along the intended planes without using force. It is worth noting that these same principles work with all juggling / spinning objects. For Changing Planes see page 64.

A **Beat, Rotation** or **(Small) Circle** is the complete rotation of the lead end of the staff on one side (End A) before coming back to its initial position. This movement is made with the wrist or hand.

A **Big Circle** or **Arm Rotation** is achieved by keeping your arms straight and moving the staff in a circle around you. This movement is made with the arm from the shoulder.

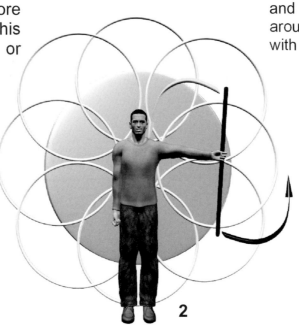

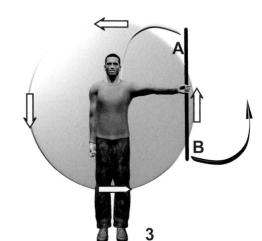

This illustration shows the theory of both big and small circles together.

Horizontal Planes

Almost all the moves in the vertical plane can also be done in the horizontal plane but it is common to find them slightly harder to do and you are more likely to hit yourself in the beginning.

Vertical Planes

The vertical plane is by far the easiest plane to learn spinning. It is much easier to handle the staff and see what you are doing.

These are the most commonly used planes for spinning, but actually there is an infinite number of planes that you can use.

Side Planes

These are the planes to your right and left:

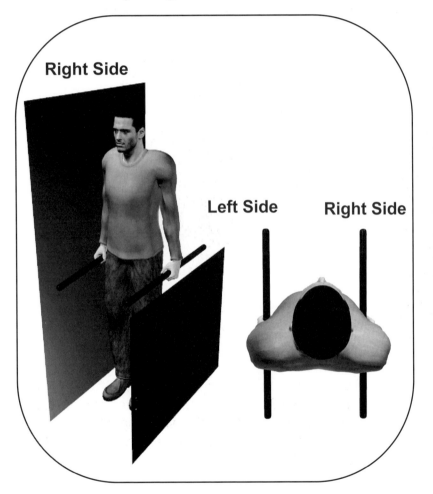

Right Side

Left Side   **Right Side**

Wall Planes

These are the planes directly in front and behind you:

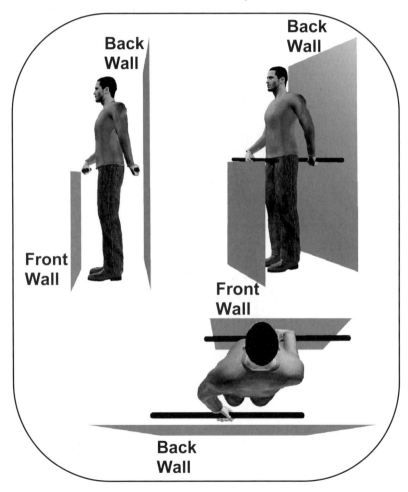

Back Wall   **Back Wall**

Front Wall

Front Wall

Back Wall

Centre Planes and Invisible Arcs

These are like side or wall planes that travel directly through you. While you learn each trick it is important to keep these planes in mind, otherwise your spinning will look sloppy and you will find it difficult to improve. Later, in the advanced sections, you will learn how to bend and change these planes when needed. (See page 64 for Plane Changes.)

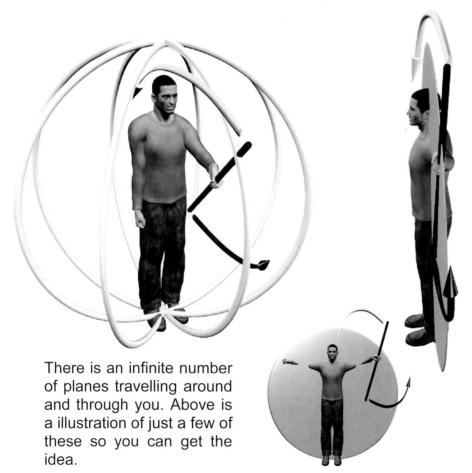

There is an infinite number of planes travelling around and through you. Above is a illustration of just a few of these so you can get the idea.

The **Central Plane** is the point which the leading end of the staff should be aiming for. This is also the crossover point for the spinning staff, which means this is the place where both ends of the staff should cross.

Circles, Beats or Rotations

Circles form the basic building blocks of spinning. They are also called 'beats' and 'rotations'.

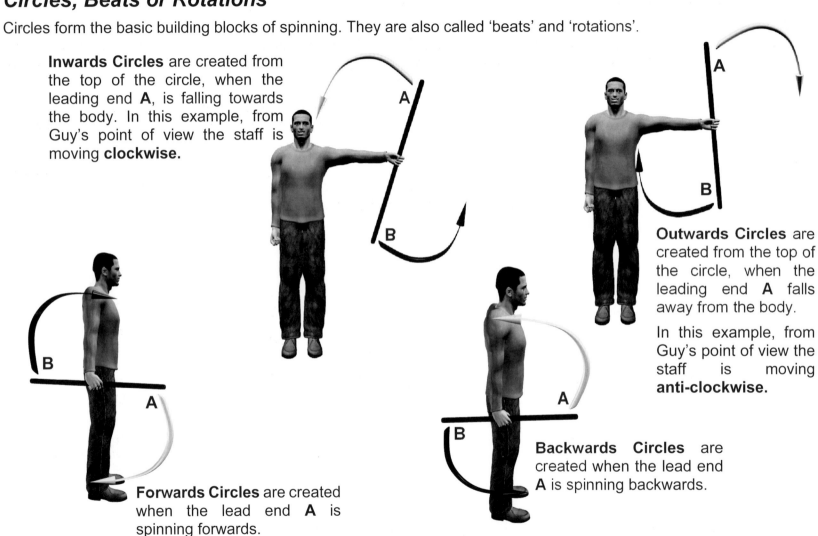

Inwards Circles are created from the top of the circle, when the leading end **A**, is falling towards the body. In this example, from Guy's point of view the staff is moving **clockwise.**

Outwards Circles are created from the top of the circle, when the leading end **A** falls away from the body.

In this example, from Guy's point of view the staff is moving **anti-clockwise.**

Forwards Circles are created when the lead end **A** is spinning forwards.

Backwards Circles are created when the lead end **A** is spinning backwards.

Forwards, Backwards, Left and Right or "F.B.L.R."

F.B.L.R. stands for Forwards, Backwards, (or Front, Back) Left and Right! It is very important that you learn each move well, (e.g. one beat circles), then learn that same move in F.B.L.R. (Forwards, Backwards, Left and Right). This may be a matter of just changing the staff direction; it might mean having to learn the trick backwards. If this doesn't make sense now, don't worry, it will become clearer once you learn a few tricks!

Once you are happy you can do the move in reverse, change hands and learn both forwards and backwards in the other hand. This will help when you want to change hands or make a transition while spinning later, as your other hand already knows what to do as well.

Finally, when you are happy doing both hands forwards and backwards, try moving the trick to another plane. Eventually, this will allow you, while spinning, to 'transition' or move in any direction you wish. Doing all this will not only make you a far better spinner, but will mean that when the time comes, you will be able to move on to double staff spinning with ease.

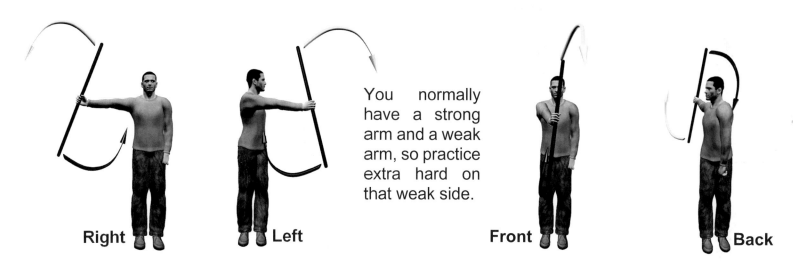

Right **Left**

You normally have a strong arm and a weak arm, so practice extra hard on that weak side.

Front **Back**

Transitions

A transition is any movement that allows you to progress from one move to another without stopping the staff. In the above illustrations the transitions of the staff go from right to left to front then back.

Basic Tricks

Hi! I'm Jessica and I will be your guide through the basic tricks section.

One Beat / Reel

a.k.a. Circles / Reel / Paddling or Half Figure of Eight

One Beats are basically continuous circles and the most basic of all the moves. They are extremely useful in linking moves and are quite simple to do. You will find that most of the movement comes from the wrist and forearm.

The staff ends never change sides like in a Figure of Eight move (see page 26), but instead, each end makes a continuous full circle on each side of your arm. It's a bit like paddling a kayak with one hand, but with much tighter circles.

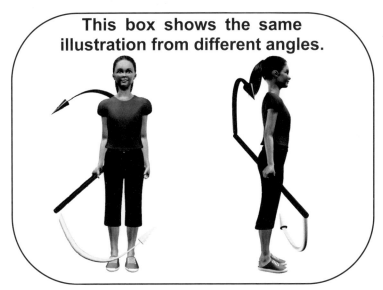

Start with the staff to your side at an angle so end B of the staff is almost touching your bottom.

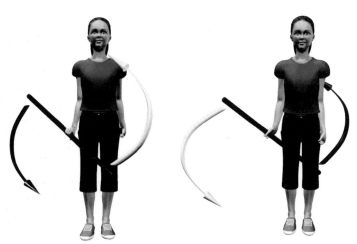

Rotate the staff with your hand / wrist making sure end B makes circles in front of you, while the following end makes circles behind you.

Tip: Try and keep your arm to your side and let your wrist do all the work for this trick.

One Beat Planes

Now try doing the same move, but with your straight arm out to your side. All the movement should be made with your wrist and a smooth rotation of your forearm. Keep your arm as straight and still as possible, also the bigger the circles, the better it looks.

Got that? Now try putting it up as high above your head as possible, remembering to keep your arm straight and using your wrist for the spinning. To maintain a good plane, from time to time you will find you have to loosen your grip a little at one point during each circle - BUT ensure your thumb and first finger grip stays tight to stop the staff from flying away.

Now if your staff isn't too long, (not longer than twice your arm length) you can try doing this move in your front plane and in your back plane. In the below example you see her facing forward spinning either backwards or forwards.

Finally, try doing the Shoulder Reel move. It's the same movement as before, but with your hand just above your shoulder right next to your ear.

It helps to keep your elbows just above shoulder hieght.

Tip: Try and keep your arm straight letting your wrist do all the work for this trick.

Don't forget to try the other hand and do the trick to your left and right sides with both hands.

Figure of Eight

- (Along a Vertical Axis) a.k.a. **The Weave**

It helps to imagine an infinity symbol ∞ or sideways 8 in front of you while performing this trick. This move is done by moving the controlling arm from side to side, while the controlling hand remains "stuck" on the staff. The idea is to paddle each end of the staff to both sides of your body creating tight circles. The trick gets this name due to the fact that the staff movement is similar to the shape of an 8 folded in on itself. Once you get this try doing it to your sides.

The action in this move is the "figure-of-eight": You want to start with the staff in a vertical position (straight up and down), arm's length to one side and in front of your body.

Start with the top end or leading end (End A) rotating forward and down and slightly to the inside, so that the bottom end (End B) passes your outside forearm.

Once end A has rotated 360 degrees from the start position, you should now be back at your original position.

Another way of explaining this move, is that you should be making a full circle with End A on the one side (i.e. inside of the arm), and then making a full circle with End A on the other side (i.e. outside of the arm.)

When you can do this move to the front, try turning your body so that the weave is to your sides.

As the staff comes down, turn to that side slightly. This move can also be done on a horizontal axis if the staff is short enough, otherwise you may hit your head.

It's a bit like rowing a boat with a paddle.

Continue end A spinning like before but instead of rotating forward, down and slightly to the inside, spin end A forward, down and slightly to the outside so that it now passes your outside forearm and end B does the spin on the inside.

Once a full spin has been made, you are back in the true starting position and can begin the cycle again. Keep your grip quite tight to begin with (you will learn where to loosen your grip and relax your hand over time) and feel the momentum of the staff, rather than forcing it around.

Hip Reel With Body Turn

a.k.a. **Reel, Carry Turn from Forwards or One Beat**

This move is the most basic way of turning around 180 degrees (or 360 if combined with another one). You will need to know how to do the One Beat (see page 23) both clockwise and anti-clockwise.

You'll need: **Small Circles, One Beat**

Dont forget try to make the step look good like a dancer!

Start by spinning some forwards circles to your side.

As the leading end of the staff (end A) goes up, step and turn 90 degrees to the left and swing the leading end past your head, letting its momentum carry it along its plane. This is also where we "carry" the turn.

Once you get that, try doing it all in the other direction. (You need to practice this with both hands too as you will be using this move a lot when you come to double staffs later.)

You should have turned a full 180 degrees from your start position by now.

Once the staff gets here it's all in the wrist again, but backwards.

As the staff comes down the other side, finish turning the other 90 degrees so you are now facing the other side.

VERY IMPORTANT: You will notice the staff travelling in backwards circles when you have changed sides and if you turn back again, the direction will change back again too. Every time you change direction, the staff spinning direction changes at the same time.

One Handed Windmill

a.k.a. Staff Fountain

The Staff Fountain is just a fancy name for a figure of eight with one hand doing F.B.L.R. This is a visually amazing move which looks harder than it really is. It involves changing from the left side to the right side of your body (in the wall plane) which makes the staff spin from a forwards to backwards figure of eight movement. Be sure you have learned the Figure of Eight with the staff spinning forwards and backwards in both the right and then the left hand. The transfer over is when End A finishes a full cycle / beat and can cross over to the other side of your body and continue the move. (It should now be spinning in the reverse direction too.) It's a very important basic side to side transfer.

You'll need: **Small Circles, One Beat, Hip Reel / Carry Turn, Figure 8's**

First, start with a Figure of Eight move, (see page 26) outwards to your side.

On the downward spin drop your arm and carry the staff to your left side.

Your feet should not move.

Let the staff rotate till the bottom end takes over as the leading end. Then spin the staff onto the far left side while continuing the spin.

This shows a continuation of the move from another angle.

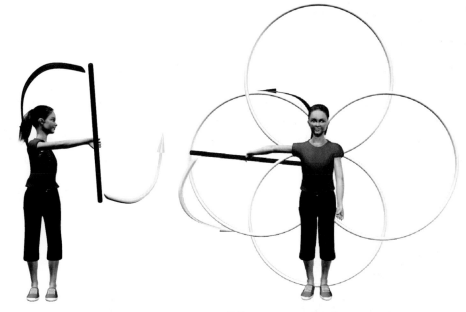

You should have noticed that when you change sides the spinning of the staff will change direction too.

On the way back to the right side you have to raise the arm to follow the Big Circle Plane.

After completing a circle on each side you should now be back where you started and ready to do it again.

Turns

- With Feet and Non-turning Moves With Body.

It is possible to change the direction of the moves by moving your feet. When changing sides it is worth keeping in mind the staff direction changes. Non-turning moves, like the one shown here are exactly the same as the turns with feet, except your feet remain firmly planted to the ground and your body / hips / torso turn to accommodate which side you want the staff to be on.

Rotors

The Rotor is the most basic Hand Exchange move that produces a smooth circle continuously in one direction on any chosen plane by passing it from hand to hand. To start with we will learn the front facing vertical rotor. It is really important here to pay close attention to what your hands are doing all the time, otherwise you will find it turning into a mess!

Facing front place both hands on the centre of the staff so both your thumbs are almost touching, palms facing down.

Let go of the left hand and turn the staff with your right hand 180 degrees clockwise, so that your palm is now facing up.

As your right hand is doing this, your left hand should be falling and crossing under your right wrist, grabbing the staff so that both your palms are now facing up.

As with all tricks practice slowly, then build up speed and remember to practice spinning both directions until it is smooth like a rotor of an airplane.

Once you get it, try spinning the staff in the other direction.

Both your thumbs should almost be touching again.

Let go of the right hand and turn the staff with your left hand another 180 degrees clockwise, so that your palms are now facing down again.

Your right hand now receives the staff again, thumbs almost touching once more so both palms are facing down. You are ready to start again...

Tip: Try and keep the staff spinning in a perfect circle / plane while spinning the Rotor.

Rotor Above the Head / Helicopter

This trick creates a horizontal circle above your head. Now, using exactly the same techniques as used in the rotor, change the plane of the rotor to above your head like a helicopter. While you learn this move take extra care with your hand exchange as you could drop the spinning staff onto your head!

You'll need: **Rotor**

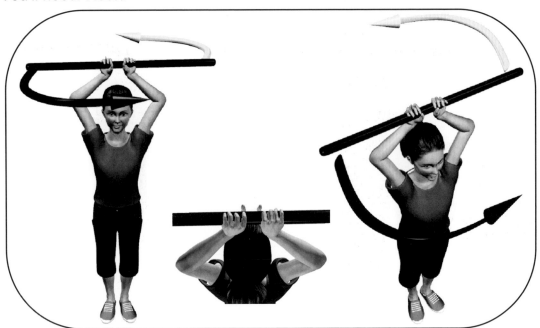

Start with the staff held above your head with your thumbs almost touching.

This view shows what's going on from above.

Remember to go slow to begin with to get the movement right. If the planes are wrong you should feel the staff going off balance.

Tip: Once you get it, try to stop looking up at your hands and remember to smile.

Tip: To add an extra twist to this move you can step / rotate / pirouette your body under the staff while continuing the Helicopter!

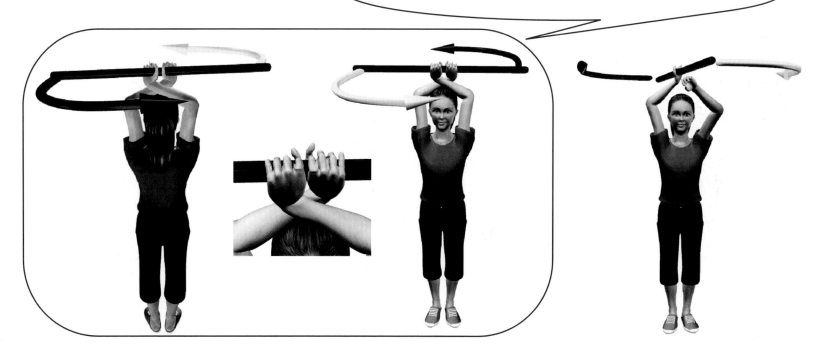

Adjust the planes so that the staff spins perfectly like a helicopter.

When your hands meet again they should always have the thumbs almost touching. If they are not you are probably doing something wrong.

When you have this running smoothly go check out how to do Palm Spins as a great addition to this move. (See page 56)

Behind The Back Rotor

Now you can do a Rotor in front, this should be quite a simple movement, in fact, the wrists don't turn and twist as much as the front rotor; it's just a pass from hand to hand. If the staff is hitting your legs or head while spinning then your wall planes are off and you might need to slow down and adjust the angle of your wrists - a mirror helps for learning this move.

Remember, once you have mastered the basics, you will notice there are various ways of doing the more advanced moves. It is important that you find what works best for you to achieve the desired result and stick with that. Learn and practice it that same way, so that when you wish to speed things up your arms will have good 'muscle memory'. This means your muscles will know what to do without you having to think about it too much.

You'll need: **Rotor**

Start by holding the staff vertical behind you so the staff is parallel with your body. The lead end A is pointing up and your palms are facing outwards.

Let go of your right hand and rotate the staff 180 degrees. Try to look straight ahead.

Lead end A should be facing down with the hand holding the staff directly in the lower small of your back. Your palms should now be facing inwards, with the staff vertical. Exchange hands making sure the left hand grabs the staff, with your palm facing inwards.

Continue the spin another 180 degrees until your right hand can grab it again and continue the process.

Horizontal Rotor Behind The Back

Once you get the hang of this "Behind The Back Rotor" try the "Horizontal Behind The Back" version. Even though it's a very similar move the effect is visually different and works really well with other horizontal moves. This move also works really well lying or kneeling on the ground.

You'll need: **Behind The Back Rotor**

Under The Leg Rotor

Yet another version of "Rotor" move. Lift your leg as the leading end is dropping and as it reaches the horizontal point of the spin, you pass the staff under your leg to the other hand, which continues the move out from under your leg. As illustrated below, the staff should stay spinning in one place and the performer's body should be doing most of the moving around. Remember to try and make it flow with other moves so that it isn't just a "trick" by itself. This trick works well both vertically and horizontally.

You'll need: **Rotor**

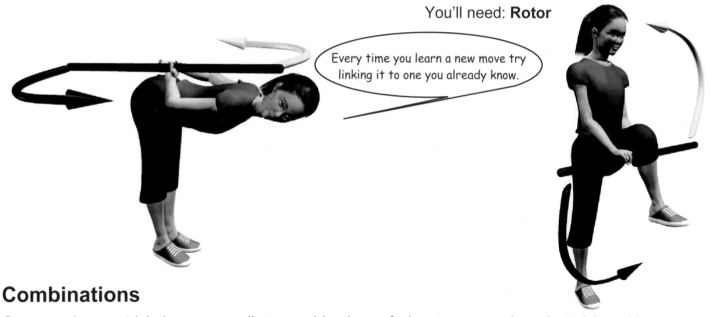

Every time you learn a new move try linking it to one you already know.

Combinations

Once you learn a trick there are endless combinations of where you can place that trick and how you combine it with the next one. Take some time to experiment and figure out these different combinations once you learn the basic theory of a move.

Behind the Back Rotor Pass

a.k.a. **Two Handed Windmill**

This vertical move is very similar to the One Handed Windmill, except that it uses both hands and a Hand Exchange / Transition. Because you use both arms it means that your body has very little turning to do. It is basically a horizontal pass behind the back, but you can also vary this move by passing in front of you as well as behind you.

You'll need: **Rotor and One Handed Windmill**

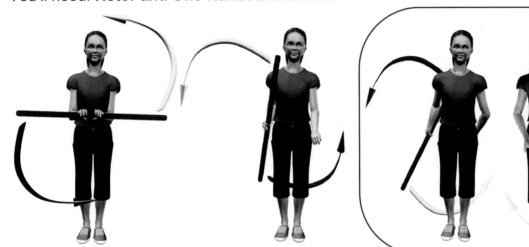
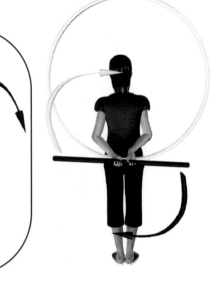

Start with a basic clockwise Rotor. (see page 32)

When the leading end A is spinning up and away from you, move the following end B to your back side, as if you were going to do a Behind the Back Rotor.

Twisting your wrist, the staff should now spin behind you. This illustration shows the same part of the move from two angles. Note your body does not turn.

Now pass / exchange the staff from one hand to the other. Your thumbs should almost be touching if you have done it correctly.

Your hands should follow the same planes as the big circle shown in the below illustrations:

Keeping your arms straight, rotate the staff (making sure that it stays in the vertical plane) up above your head.

Now, above your head with straight arms, grab / exchange the staff back to your other hand. Once again your thumbs should almost be touching.

You have a choice at this point to continue the rotation of the staff behind you to repeat the move, or transition the staff to the front to continue where you started in a Rotor.

360 Exchange

a.k.a. **Rotor 360 / Rotor with Body Turn**

The aim of this trick is to keep the staff spinning the Rotor move in one place while you rotate. It is a very useful way of moving around.

You'll need: **Rotor, Turns**

Be graceful! Don't forget to make the step and turn look good like a dancer!

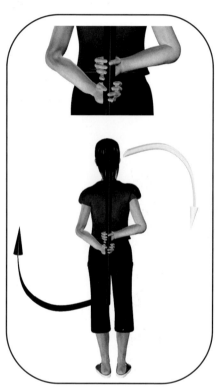

Start with the Rotor move spinning in an anti-clockwise direction.

When this is working smoothly, take the staff in the right hand as normal but, as you do, turn your body 180 degrees away from the staff so that the left hand can take the staff behind your back.

Both palms should be facing out when you pass the staff from one hand to the other, much like the hand exchange in the Behind the Back Rotor.

The staff should not move orientation or change plane while you are doing this move. Don't get too caught up in what the hands are doing, instead keep your body spinning on the spot and let your hands figure it out. When they do, remember to practice it that way till you feel you have it. As a rough guide, the staff should spin 1 or 1½ times for each 180 degrees you rotate.

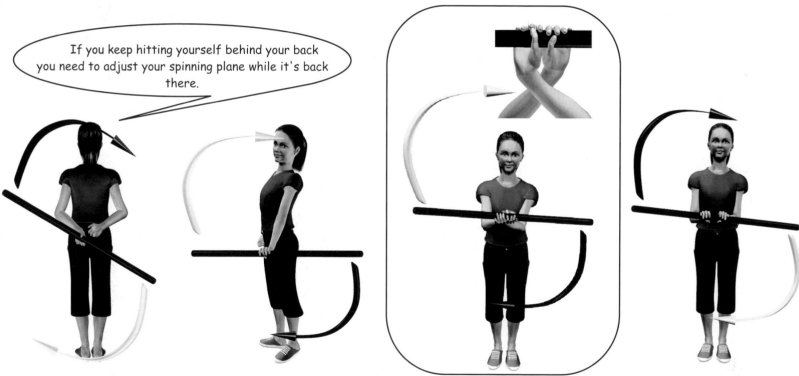

If you keep hitting yourself behind your back you need to adjust your spinning plane while it's back there.

Now it's time to finish with the left side...

Bring your left hand round to complete the spin and turn your body the rest of the 90 degrees to complete the turn.

You should now be facing front again right where you started while keeping the Rotor spinning.

d Weave

similar to the Weave or Figure of Eight moves, but uses both hands as in the Rotor
s your staff from one side to the other really well - making it a great linking trick.

w example is done with the staff spinning backwards. This will help when learning the
Num. nuck move on page 44. Don't forget to learn it spinning forwards too!

You'll need: **Small Circles, One Beats, Figure 8's**

Remember to try and keep your arms and your hand exchanges centred between your shoulders.

The first hand should be making a full circle with End A on the one side (inside of the arm), and then making a full circle with End A on the other side (outside of the arm).

At this point the free hand goes under the other wrist and grabs the staff.

Then the other hand does the exact same thing after taking the staff like the technique used in the Rotor move. (See page 32)

This is the view from the left side.

Use the same hand exchange technique as shown in the Rotor move to get back to the right side again.

Finally, back to where you started.

Extra Spins

As you become more advanced, you will want to put in some extra spins. They look great and are achieved when you twist up your wrist / hand / arm during a figure of eight to get more rotations out of the staff. For example, with a figure of eight move, you get a complete circle with each end of the staff. A Double Spin (a.k.a. Shotgun, or Snake) will get an extra circle out of each end of the staff on the side it's on, hence the name.

To get extra beats (read Circles and Beats page 20) from the staff without passing it from hand to hand try **Palm Spinning** (see page 56) or **Finger Spinning** (see page 63). Try twisting your wrist and arm up on both sides of your body to get an extra half circle on both sides, this will give an extra beat to the entire movement on each side.

Moves

...oves work best with longer staffs as you need to have room to grab the end. This move is similar to the ...d Weave, found on the previous page. Passing it up and over your arm is the easiest variant. Use your other ...asp it from under your armpit and repeat the process on the other side. Unlike many moves, you may find this ...your hand holds are slightly off centre on the staff.

First hold the staff in front of you with a straight arm, leading end A facing up.

Rotate the staff up and over your shoulder, while your other hand reaches for the staff under your armpit.

At this point the passing arm will lock (not go any further). With your other hand, reaching under your armpit, grab the staff with your thumb facing up.

This is also a great place to pause for dramatic impact!

Now let go of the top hand and allow the bottom grabbing hand to continue the rotation of the staff up and over to repeat on the opposite side.

When you get that try it in reverse. Passing it up and under your arm is a little harder, but made easier by a small push at the end.

Here is another great place to pause for dramatic impact!

Rotate the staff up and over your shoulder, while your other hand reaches for the staff under your armpit and grabs it.

Once again let go of the top hand and allow the bottom grabbing hand to finish the rotation of the staff. At this point you should find yourself back where you started, ready to go again.

Tip: Remember as soon as you learn a new move or trick, try to teach it to a friend. The more you teach something the better you become at it!

Kick Ups

These are great when you are learning and dropping the staff a lot. Rather then bending down to pick up the staff, you can use a kick up.

Non-spinning Kick Ups

The first and most popular is the "Pull / Kick" version. Starting with the staff on the ground, place your foot on the centre of the staff, pull back and push down with your foot and with one fluid motion, pointing your toe to the ground to allow the staff to roll up onto the foot a bit. At this point, kick the staff up to the desired catch point. If this is a bit too tricky, it also works well to use the other foot to push or roll the staff onto the kicking foot, much like a hackie sack.

You can also do a "Foot Catch Kick Up" or "Toe Delay", which is basically where you catch it with your foot (instead of letting it drop to the ground), exactly like you would do with a hackie sack and kick it back up. For comfort, you may want to wear sturdy shoes while learning this trick!

Smoothly lift your foot ready for the catch.

As the staff connects, lower the foot gently to cushion the impact. This will help slow its speed and keep it balanced for the kick back.

Spinning Kick Ups

Another type of Kick Up is one used by club jugglers who drop clubs. To do this you must use one foot to help lay the staff correctly on the launching / kicking foot. Once ready, sharply lift your foot up, trapping the staff between your shin and foot causing it to fly up already spinning. This never works first time because the staff slips out of this delicate arrangement, so be patient.

Start by resting the staff two thirds of the way up across your right foot so that the long end is laying on the floor in front of you at a slight angle.	**Now roll your right foot / ankle over to the right or to the outside and raise your toes up. You're ready for the kick up!**	**Kick your right foot up towards your left shoulder, keeping your foot twisted with your toes stretching up. The staff should get caught between your right foot and shin.**	**When you get this careful balance correct, the staff should spin up in a horizontal plane. If the plane is wrong, adjust the angle your foot kicks up.**	**Once you have the kick up correct, the staff should be easy to grab and allow you to go straight into spinning.**

Tip: It also helps to wear rubber edged shoes with this one.

Balancing a Stick / Cane / Umbrella

Looking for something fun to do to start a show? How about pulling some sweet tricks while balancing stick tricks? All these moves work well with a cane or umbrella act too. (Please see page 95).

First place the end of your staff firmly in the palm of your dominant hand.

Slowly take your non-dominant hand off the shaft, making sure to keep the stick as vertical as possible. The key to this trick is to keep an eye on the top half of the staff to help see which way you need to compensate. The more you practice this the longer you will be able to keep it balanced.

Practice! You won't be great the first time you try! Behind every great trick are a hundred failed attempts.

Once you find it easy, try some tricks! Be creative! See if you can put this a trick into a combo of moves, moving as fluidly from one trick to the next as you can. Easier said than done!

There really are no boundaries and nothing's keeping you from creating your own signature move.

Tip: Remember the key to balancing anything is to watch the top of the item you are balancing and adjust accordingly.

Balance Tricks

Here's a few to get you going:

Backhand: Balancing the stick in your dominant palm, push the stick into the air. In mid-flight, flip your hand over so your stick butt lands on the back of your hand. Remember to push your stick up in such a way that it lands vertically. Also, try to have your hand absorb a little of the impact by moving your hand slightly down as your stick lands.

Around the World: Balancing anywhere on your head, start rotating your whole body. You will have to tilt your stick into the turn slightly to keep it balanced. See how many times you can go around the world! This can be done on your hand too and is probably an easier way to start.

Hand-to-Hand: Balance your stick, then gently hop it to your other hand. See how many times you can go hand to hand! Be careful not to go too fast and be sure to regain your balance between each hop or your stick will lose its balance and fall. Can also be done backhand.

Piano Fingers: Balance your stick on one or two fingers.

The Insult: Balance your stick on any 'insulting' part of your body!

Thumbs Up: Balance your stick on the tip of your vertically extended thumb.

Head Job: Balance your stick on any part of your head.

Foot Job: Balance your stick on your foot.

Tandem: With a friend, go hand to hand between the two of you. Feeling daring? Try it with two sticks! Can be done backhand as well.

The Flip: Just as it sounds, balance your stick, flip it up in the air, and catch it balanced. Can be done backhand, but only if you're really daring!

Intermediate Moves

My name's Brad. Well done for getting through the basics. That's the hardest bit done now!

Rolls / Wraps / Spins

This set of moves is a good starting point for learning contact style staff spinning. Contact staff spinning is a way of manipulating the staff with every part of your body. (Not just your hands).

Wrist / Hand Roll

This is great for changing direction of the staff when needed.

You'll need: **Small Circles, One Beats**

Moving your arm slightly from left to right helps the staff roll smoothly and keeps your hand in the centre of the staff.

Start facing front, place one hand to the right of the centre of the staff with your palm facing down.

Spin your leading end 180 degrees up and over, so that your palm is now facing up.

Open your hand slightly, letting the staff rotate fully so that your thumb is the last part of your hand still holding the staff.

Just as it leaves your thumb, let it continue to spin. At the same time, rotate your hand the opposite way to the staff to catch the staff as it rolls over the back of your hand.

Once you have the staff gripped firmly in your hand, keep it going and do another. With practice, you should be able to get this really smooth.

51

Neck Roll

This move allows you to roll the staff behind your neck from one side to the other.

This can be done two ways - with the same hand both releasing and catching the staff, or with one hand releasing and the other hand catching. The two handed or second version is shown below as this is easier to start with and will give you more control.

Start with the staff spinning in the front plane, with the releasing hand gripping the staff about one hand width away from the centre.

Bend your neck slightly forward and rotate the staff so that your hand ends up on the side of your neck. The centre of the staff should pass over the back of your neck.

Now, let go and let the momentum of the staff carry itself over your neck.

Finally grab the staff with the other hand on the other side of your neck as it rotates round and finish off where you started.

To do this with only one hand, you must be fast enough to release the staff on one side of your neck and then get that hand round to the other side for the catch. To help with control, try to roll the staff slowly to begin as this will give you a bit more time for the catch. With a bit of practice and patience you will manage this fine. Try doing the trick both ways and then try changing the side and directions you come into it from.

Back Rolls / Back Spins

Back Rolls are very similar to Neck Rolls except the staff rolls across your back.

Like the Neck Roll, this can be done as the one handed version or as the easier two handed version, shown below. Don't forget to learn it both sides so you can link to a move in any direction you wish.

Start with the staff spinning in the front plane, with the releasing hand gripping the staff about one hand width away from the centre.	**Leaning forwards a bit, hold your left arm close to your side and pass the staff around your torso and onto your back.**	**Allow the momentum of the staff to roll over your back while trying to keep it in the vertical plane.**	**When the staff has rolled over your back, use your other hand to grab it as it comes to the vertical position by your other side.**	**Finally straighten up again to bring the staff back to the beginning position.**

Tip: This trick can be applied to any part of your body, such as your arms, legs or even your head!

Elbow Roll

a.k.a. **The Conveyor Belt**

The Elbow Roll is a lovely move that is simple once you understand the sequence. This contact move has the staff roll over the elbow, and then up and over the wrist. In the example shown, use the right hand as the release / starting hand and the left elbow / hand for receiving the staff.

Start with the staff in the front plane spinning clockwise. Your hand should be slightly off centre to the right.

When end A is coming up, bend your other arm's elbow.

The leading end comes up so that your leading thumb and receiving elbow touch. As the staff continues the spin, its centre should connect with your elbow at which point you release the staff from the lead hand.

It will continue to spin over your elbow until end A connects with your outside forearm.

It is much harder to get this trick moving in reverse but if contact style spinning is your thing then you might want to put the time in to learn it F.B.L.R. (see page 21.) There are also many other combinations you can try from here. Why not experiment a bit, maybe see how any of the moves you already know could link into this move. Then see what tricks you know that will link after this move.

When the spin connects with your forearm, move your forearm forwards slightly to balance the staff while it does the last spin.

As it comes round push your arm out slightly more, opening your hand for the catch. This is where the wrist / hand roll over happens to get it to your hand.

Catch the staff and continue spinning!

Palm Spins

Just as the name suggests, Palm Spins are when you let go of the staff and allow the momentum of the staff to continue spinning on the palm of your hand. The other hand only serves to boost the movement / speed as needed. This move looks nice with short staffs in front of your body or done above the head with a long staff, usually starting out as the Helicopter.

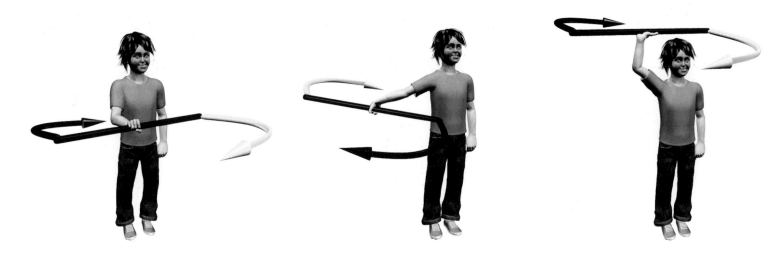

Start with your lead hand in the centre of the staff with the palm facing down.

Now rotate the staff like you were about to start the Helicopter move. (But don't get your other hand in the way).

Tip: You can also start this move very easily from the Helicopter move. (See page 34)

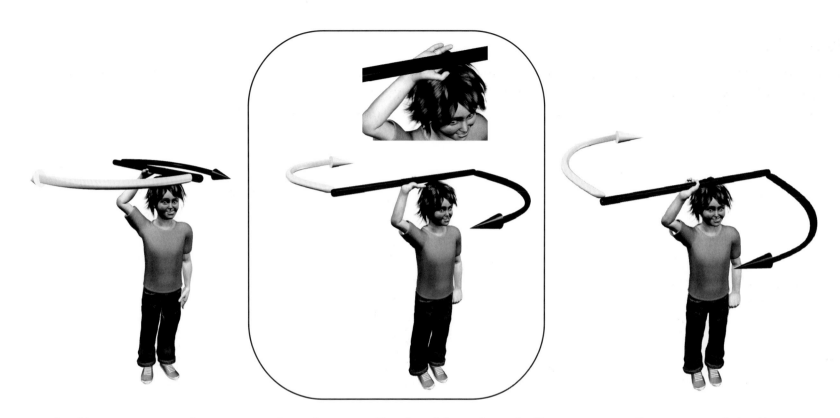

As it comes up above your head, open the lead hand and allow the staff's momentum to continue spinning on your flat upturned palm. To help keep it balanced, try to hold your palm as horizontal as possible.

Got this? Try Palm Spins lying on your back.

As you get better at this you will be able to use the other hand to keep the spin going indefinitely, a bit like spinning a basketball.

Throws

There are so many variations of staff throwing, but all that really matters is that you catch them! It's worth mentioning that the more controlled your throws are, the easier your catches will be. As you get better at these standard throws, try different combinations. If you are worried about getting hit on the head, wearing a bike helmet can help your confidence!

Palm Spin Throw

This trick looks really nice and can be adapted to different planes. When you feel it is right and balanced make a sharp push up which will launch the horizontally spinning staff into the air. Catching it is the hard part!

Get the Palm Spin spinning really smoothly above your head. It is really important to have the staff perfectly balanced in the centre and rotating in a perfectly horizontal plane.

Once you have the perfect Palm Spin going push your arm straight up and let the momentum of the staff do the rest.

Once the staff is airborne, keep an eye on it so you can prepare for the catch. If you're not ready it could hurt!

Catch the staff firmly allowing it to continue to rotate into your next move.

Tip: Be careful while learning this move, as if you miss the catch you can often get hit on the head.

Rotation with Launcher Throw

The idea is the same as the Rotor move, except that you perform the all the movements with one hand. This is the easiest throw to do with a staff as the staff is spinning on a vertical plane.

Start with the staff in the front plane spinning clockwise.	**Rotate the staff in the direction you wish to throw. In this example he spins and throws clockwise.**	**When the hand is turned skyward and your wrist is unable to twist any further, release the staff, allowing its momentum to give controlled airborne spin.**	**Spin your hand round, ready to catch it in the horizontal position.**	**Finally, catch it with your palm turned down and to the right, continuing the rotation back to the start position.**

Tip: Try to keep the throw small and controlled to begin with, it will make the catches easier. As you get better spin higher and faster for more difficulty.

Throwing Exchanges

This is exactly the same as throwing and catching with one hand (see page 59), but instead you use the other hand to do the catching, (see illustrations below). You can throw the staff from your left hand to the right hand and vice versa.

Once you have mastered a basic throw, you might like to try one of these variations:

One spin in the air before catching. (As above).

More than one spin. (Higher throws).

Throws in both the vertical and horizontal plane.

Spinning faster, slower or not at all.

Palm Spins Throws, see page 58 for Palm Spinning.

Try catching the centre of staff on top of your foot and then kicking it back up for the hand grab. (See page 46 for Kick Ups).

Try to catch the end of staff on your foot and throw it back up using your foot and ankle as a lever, (juggling club style).

Throwing Game

The Throwing Game is a little game of catch I made up when there were other staff throwers around that wanted to practice throwing and catching.

Basically, the game involves doing a trick, then throwing the staff to the next person who repeats the first trick and adds a trick of their own. He or she then throws the staff back to you or the next spinner, who must repeat the previous two tricks and add yet another. With each turn, the catcher repeats the previous tricks and adds another. Any player who drops the staff or fails to copy the trick sequence is out.

There are 3 rules below which you can add one at a time for each person as they feel ready, allowing the game difficulty to increase at an appropriate speed for all players. This is good if you have an advanced thrower (who is happy with all three rules) who wants to play with a beginner thrower (who might want only rule one to apply to him).

Rule 1:

Only front facing vertical throws can be made.

Rule 2:

Both front and side vertical throws can be made.

Rule 3:

All throws including horizontal Helicopter and Palm Spin Throws are allowed.

Advanced Moves

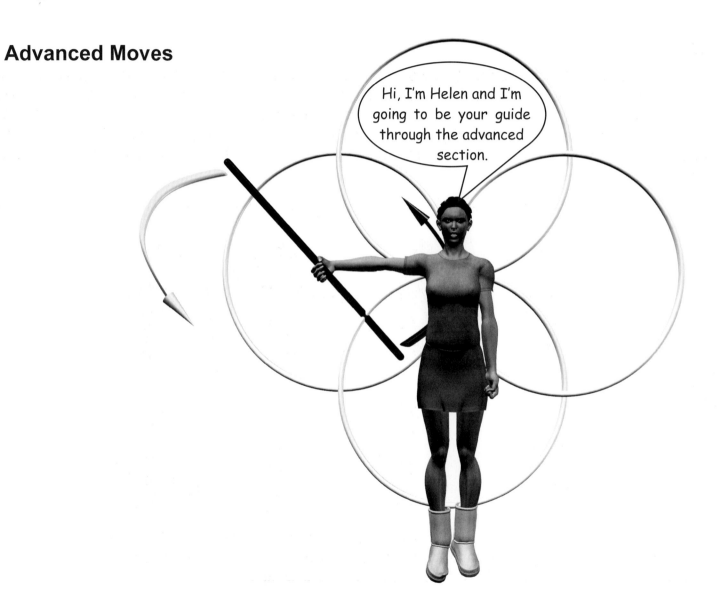

Finger Spins

This technique allows you to add extra spins at almost any time to any move you can do. Some people think this is basic, but I would hold off learning any finger spinning moves until you are comfortable with the moves in the intermediate section. It is really important to master the basics before you complicate the moves with extra spins and finger placement, but if you feel you are ready, they are very useful to learn. It's harder to do with thicker staffs, as the staff centre needs to comfortably fit between your fingers, just like spinning a pen through your fingers.

This is one way of doing it, but obviously you should learn it in the opposite direction and with all fingers on both hands.

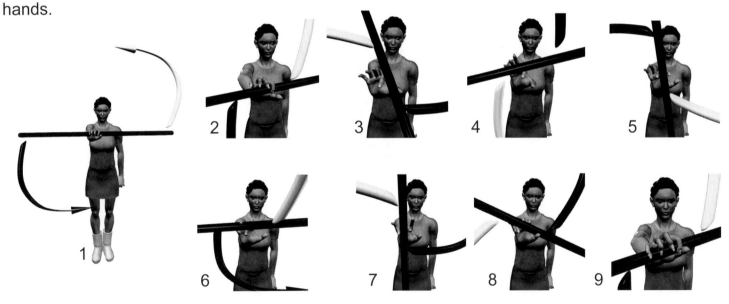

First use each finger (staff should roll between each finger) in turn. The thumb is very important because it gives the force needed for the staff to turn. Most people don't use their pinky finger as it is not normally strong enough.

Plane Changes

By now you should fully understand how planes work and why we use them. (If you don't, go to page 16.) Learning how to change planes drastically or gently will give you even more freedom in your movement and trick combinations.

There are a few different Plane Change methods to choose from:
1) Forcing the change of plane.
2) Using a contact style move to roll the staff from one plane to another.
3) Stopping and then starting in a new plane. (Please see the following illustrations for an example of this.)

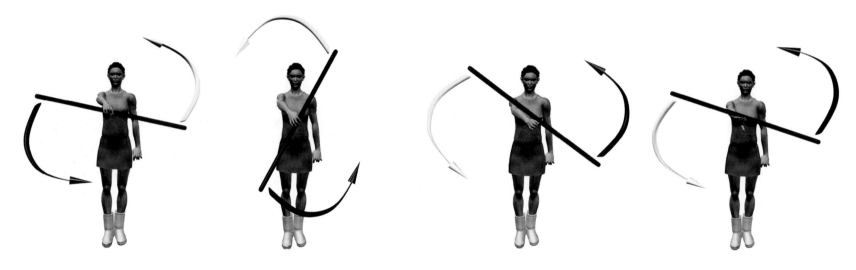

Start with the staff spinning in the front plane.

This shows the Hand Roll (see page 51) move and how it is one of many tricks you can use to go into a Plane Change.

Try finding different tricks you can Plane Change into and out of.

The below illustrations show a Hand Roll / Wrap (see page 51), spinning in a vertical plane (see page 17). Using the "Stop and then Start" method she finds a good place to stop and then continues into a horizontal plane (see page 17). It is important to make the stops look intentional and sharp. A sloppy, wrongly angled stop looks bad so pay close attention.

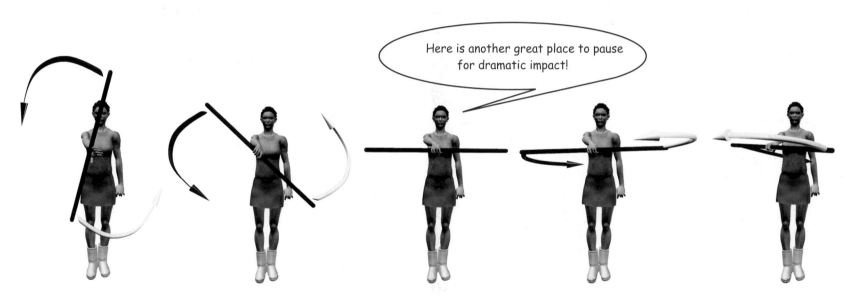

Here is another great place to pause for dramatic impact!

As the momentum takes the staff over the back of your wrist, roll your hand over to grab it again.

Grasp the staff firmly again, continuing the rotation.

Once the staff reaches a perfectly level position, stop it still with a firm handgrip.

Now you can change the staff's spinning plane and carry on in a completely different direction.

Halo Roll

a.k.a. Simple SNS

This is a slightly harder contact move to learn. The staff rolls from one shoulder to the other on the vertical plane. To begin with try not to go too fast as it will hurt when it hits you, or too slow as it will fall off.

Leaning forwards slightly, grip the staff under your armpit and push it up clockwise and over your shoulder.

The staff should stay in contact with your body the entire time. (This is why it's called a contact move.)

Push it up towards your head, and let it rotate between your shoulder blades.

Tip: Be careful not to go too fast to begin with as the staff will fly off or, worse, hit you.

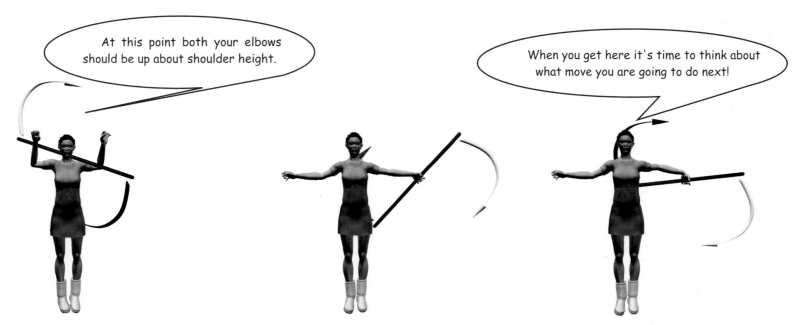

After the rotation the staff will just rotate / fall naturally towards your other shoulder where you should let it come slightly over the shoulder and catch the falling end in the armpit / left hand.

Combining Moves

When picking and choosing your favourite moves it is important to keep in mind that linking the moves is just as important as the two tricks you're trying to link. You can also combine one and two handed moves to create unique and exciting moves. Every time you learn a new trick spend some time figuring out how to link it to your existing moves. This will also mean that you'll discover many new things along the way. As there are hundreds of tricks that you can link with other tricks it makes this learning process a never-ending and addictive hobby. Experiment, have fun, try things out, just remember your planes and how the motion of the staff works. Try everything with different speeds and directions to see what happens.

Isolations

Isolations freeze all or parts of the staff, changing the points of where the staff rotates.

Mime Style: Pretend the staff won't move (i.e. locked in the air) while you move around it.

Off Centre Rotation: The staff normally spins where your hand grips it, but it doesn't have to! You can change the point the staff spins around just by isolating that one spot. (Freezing that part of the staff to that place.) In the illustrations below the staff is isolated at one end so the rest of the staff must rotate from this point.

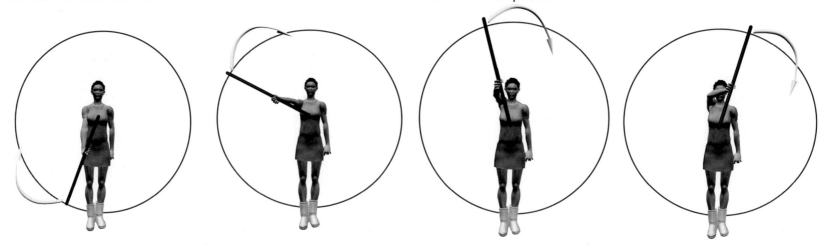

It is important to really hold that isolated point in the same place while everything else moves around that point. It helps to practice this move in front of a mirror so you can see yourself moving and adjust accordingly.

Tip: Every bit of the staff can be isolated to create infinite combinations. Depending on where your hand placement is on the staff can change it all again!

Fishtails

This is a relatively easy contact move where the staff makes a one beat Figure of Eight, while balancing on the back of your hand and moving the arm from side to side. When you first learn to do this, it is useful to use your other hand to guide the staff while it's on the back of your main hand (to avoid hitting yourself too much). When you feel ready you can remove this guide hand. Try to do this move as slowly as you can to remain in control. Fishtails are easier to learn in reverse, as illustrated below, but as always, remember to practice both hands and forwards as well.

Start by holding the staff like a kayak paddle and start a backwards One Beat.

When you're ready, roll the staff over the back of the hand. The staff should roll from your little finger end of the hand to the thumb.

Once you have completed the palm roll on to the back of your hand, take the staff to the opposite side of your body using the back of your hand.

Keep the centre of the staff as balanced as possible while your hand moves it side to side.

Now you have learned the idea of Fishtails try doing it with different parts of your hands, arms and body. When you can perform this smoothly try turning 360 degrees with a Fishtail. It can be done!

Head Spins

This trick uses similar techniques to Palm Spinning, except it is a bit more difficult to keep the staff spinning flat and balanced on top of your head.

If you can do 2 or 3, you are doing really well; with practice you may get many more spins.

First, using your right hand hold the staff slightly off centre so the middle of the staff is a few inches from your thumb.

Spin anticlockwise and horizontal, making sure that you keep your eyes on the centre of the staff as it approaches your head.

When you place the rotating staff onto your head try to get it right on the centre of the staff otherwise it will just fly off. See if you can get it to rotate a whole spin before having to catch it.

Try to take the staff off your head with your left hand before it falls off, otherwise you will have to catch the staff where it falls off.

Anti-Spin

Anti-Spin makes the rotation point move in an opposite direction circle to the direction the staff is spinning in. The illustration below shows a Windmill trick (see page 30) in Anti-Spin style. It might feel a little strange at first, but once you learn the idea behind Anti-Spin you can apply it to almost any trick to make new and wonderful patterns.

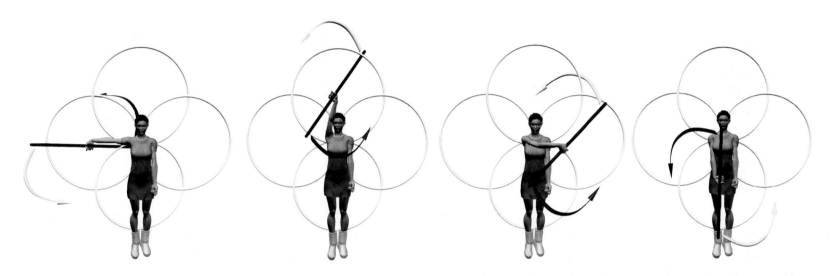

Begin by spinning a normal Windmill (see page 30). When you are in a smooth rhythm, come back to the start position, and make an extra beat on that side.

This extra beat allows you to change the direction of your arm movement to the other direction, while keeping the staff rotation the same direction it started in.

Tip: Make sure you can do the trick really well before attempting to anti-spin it!

Double Staff Moves

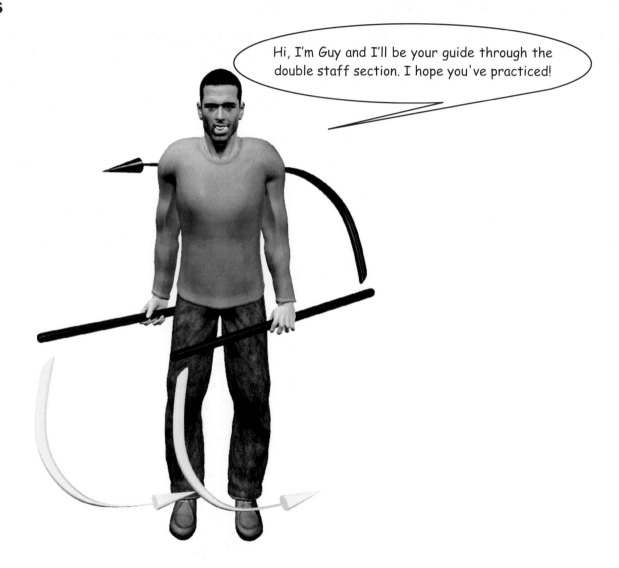

So you think you're ready for Double Staffs?

If you have made it this far (or even jumped ahead) and you feel confident, now is a good time to pick up another staff. I would recommend using two shorter staffs for this section (see page 11 for staff selections).

The golden rule here is good technique, not speed - it's better to look slow and in sync than fast and sloppy!

Remember, getting your hands to do two different things at the same time is hard at first. If things get too complicated, stop, put one staff down and practice more with the hand that seems to be having a problem. When you know this you can fix it, pick up your other staff and continue on your merry way.

At this point you will also understand why it was so important to learn all of the single staff moves in both hands, on all sides and in both directions.

From this point I will assume you have completed all the concepts covered in the previous sections in F.B.L.R. (see page 21). If you get stuck on a double staff move, just remember, all of these double staff moves can be broken down into moves from the previous sections; so don't forget to put one down and go back to the basics and figure out why one or both hands aren't working.

In Time or Split Time?

When you start to learn spinning with two staffs, you will have to decide if you want to have them running In Time (Parallel or Non Parallel) or out of time, known as Split Time (one then the other) - when you have finished learning one way try the other. This will allow you to have twice as many moves and much more freedom to turn.

In Time spinning means the leading ends of the staffs both reach the bottom of their circles at the same time. They should be doing the same thing at the same time in both hands. The staffs can either be travelling in the same direction (parallel) or opposite directions, (NOT parallel).

Split Time is different to this because the leading end of the staffs take turns to reach the bottom of their circles. The staffs are always exactly half a circle / spin apart.

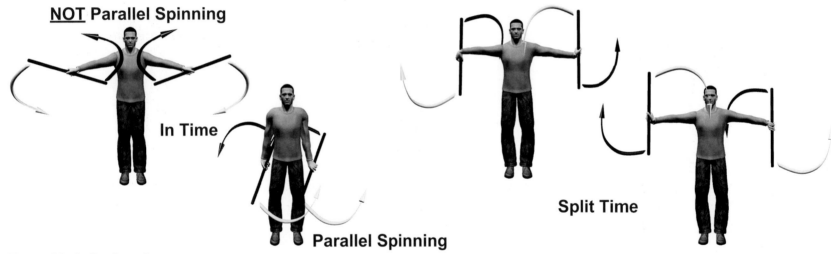

NOT Parallel Spinning

In Time

Parallel Spinning

Split Time

Parallel Spinning

Parallel spinning is where the leading ends of both staffs reach the bottom of their circles at the same time, or In Time. The staffs spin in parallel, that is, they are synchronised all the way round the trick.

One Beat Side Arm Reel

This is exactly the same as the One Handed Reel (see page 23) except now both hands must work together to do the same thing at the same time. The staffs spin in parallel, both making a circle in front of you and behind you in the wall planes. Although both staffs are travelling in the same direction, take note that your right hand is spinning outwards circles and your left hand is spinning inwards circles. It is really important to try to keep them both moving at the same speed and planes otherwise it will look sloppy.

You'll need: **Inwards and Outwards Circles and Reels**

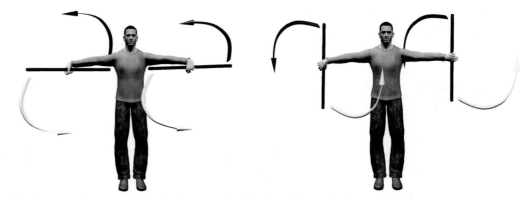

With your arms to your sides start with both staffs perfectly parallel. Now spin small circles both together at the exact same speed.

Using only your wrists try to keep the circles as tight as possible. Make sure you try this both forwards and backwards.

Tip: Use your good hand as a lead hand so you can concentrate on your weak hand. If you get stuck, stop the good hand and work on the problem hand, then, use both hands again when you've fixed the problem. Move slowly at first as you figure out what's going on.

One Beat Hip Reel

Like the Single Beat Side Arm Reel, both staffs' leading ends spin a circle in front of you and the staffs' following ends make a circle behind you. Practice with one hand first then try with both hands together. As with all reels all the movement is done with your wrists / hands, not your arms. Remember to try to keep them perfectly parallel.

You'll need: **Inwards and Outwards Circles and Reels**

With both arms / hands placed at your hips, point the staffs parallel to your sides. The leading ends should both be in front, while the following ends are at the back.

Now scoop the staffs down to your toes and around. Your right hand should be spinning outwards circles and your left hand spinning inwards circles.

Once you are comfortable with one beats, you can add more beats by doing figure of eight hip reels.

One Beat Shoulder Reels

Essentially the same as Hip and Side Arm Reels, both staffs should spin a perfectly parallel circle behind you and in front of you. If you have problems with this remember to practice with the weak hand first then add the other staff when ready.

You'll need: **Inwards and Outwards Circles and Reels.**

It helps to keep your elbows up.

Raise your arms so your hands are just above your shoulders and ears. They should not move much from here as all the movement is done with your wrists / hands.

Remember, try to keep them perfectly parallel and spinning at the same speed. A mirror can help to check your technique and make it look sharp.

Tip: Reels feel strange at first, even if you're doing them perfectly. As your wrists become more flexible you will feel this move flow more smoothly.

Butterfly

The staffs spin a circle in opposite directions either side of your body. This gives a visual illusion of you having wings. You can spin either One Beats (see page 23) or you can spin Figure of Eights (see page 26) to have faster circles. This move also looks really nice both in and out of time. If you have mastered the moves on page 75, then you can actually already do this!

You'll need: **Inwards and Outwards Circles, One Beats and Figure of Eights**

Hold both staffs out directly to your sides at shoulder height and have both arms spin Figure of Eights (see page 26) in opposite directions.

For the best visual effect, make sure you get the planes of the circles really flat!

Buzz-Saw

To do this trick you will need staffs short enough to spin circles in front of you with both arms up. They must not touch your body when holding the centre of the staff in front you, as illustrated on page 12.

When you are happy you are not going to hurt yourself, lift both of your arms up in front of your shoulders and spin One Beats or Figure of Eights in both hands making sure they stay in their own planes. This trick should be learned in both Split Time and In Time as they each produce very different effects.

You'll need: **Small Circles, One Beats and Figure of Eights**

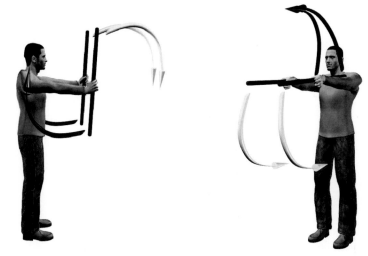

Keep your arms straight out at shoulder height directly in front of you.

The staffs should spin tight enough circles to fit between your arms. Make sure you practice this both forwards and backwards.

Tip: When performing this trick think about the angles of the audience and you. The Buzz-Saw looks much better from the side than the front!

Crossover

This move is basically two vertical One Beats where the two staffs literally cross over each other and their arcs are intertwined. At first they may crash into each other a bit, but if you make one hand the lead hand which is milliseconds out of time with the other hand, it will work.

Another really good variant of this X crossover is trying it in front or behind your body.

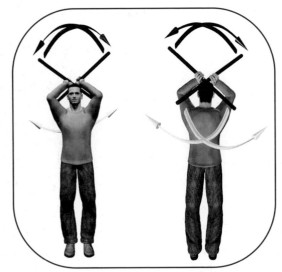

Start with staffs in an X shape held above your head, touching each other at their centres. The leading ends should make circles behind you while the following ends are making circles in front

Try to keep your hands resting on your head so that your wrists roll around doing all the work. Remember you can practice this both forwards and backwards to prepare yourself for combination with other tricks.

Tip: Remember, this move is all in the wrists. You can even do this through your legs. Be careful!

Take-out Sequences

This set of moves can be done for any double staff move that you can think of. It is really just a term used to describe when one hand stays spinning where it is and the other hand is 'taken out' to a different place / plane. The Take-out hand then may continue flowing back to where it started or on to another movement. Try doing this with a double Buzz-Saw move (see page 79).

First get them both spinning a really good Buzz-Saw in front of you. (See page 79).

As your leading ends come down to the front of you get ready for the Take-out!

When you're ready, keep your left hand spinning the Buzz-Saw and let your right hand spin down to your right and onto the opposite side to which it started.

From this position you could either bring the other hand over to meet it or just bring the Take-out hand back again.

Turning With Two Staffs

This is exactly like we did with the one staff version of this move. Once you learn the concept of turning with two staffs you can explore other ways of using this trick. How about trying it with your arms out straight to your sides? Or turning while doing the Shoulder Reel?

Be graceful! Try to make the step and turn look good like a dancer!

Start by spinning Hip Reels (see page 23). When the leading ends are coming down towards your toes, get ready to turn.

When the staffs start to travel up from your toes, step / turn 90 degrees to your left.

As you complete your turn / step, the staffs will follow over, changing the direction of their spin.

You should now be facing the other way with both staffs still spinning in a reverse Hip Reel. (Now you know why it is so important to learn both forwards and backwards.)

Tip: Be aware that from your point of view the staffs change direction when you turn, but for the audience the staffs still spin the same way.

Double Staff Throws

Once again these are just a slight variation to the single staff throws, so I will explain the basics to you, but it's probably better just to experiment with the endless combinations of staff throws. Essentially you can either throw and catch with the same hand, or throw with one hand and catch with the other. The illustration below shows the latter type - a throw with one hand, passing of the non-thrown staff between hands above the head, then a catch with the opposite hand.

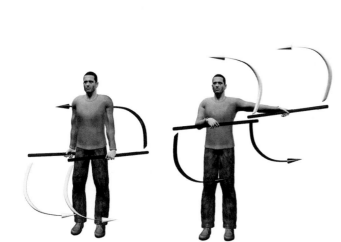  

Start this trick in a classic Hip Reel move (see page 23).

When the staffs are moving up from your feet, bend your right arm to the left and straighten your left arm to the left. Keep your staffs spinning in parallel.

As soon as your right hand locks, throw the staff in a vertical spin (see page 58 for throwing a staff). While this is happening continue spinning your left hand up back towards your head for the hand exchange. As the thrown staff reaches the peak of its throw you should exchange hands and get ready to catch it with your left hand.

While you make the catch with your left hand, your right hand should be continuing the spin of the other staff back down to the start position.

The "Drought" of Moves

In time you will come to a place where you feel a bit stuck, like you have run out of moves and ideas. Don't worry, this always passes; maybe take a break from staff spinning and go looking for some new inspiration.

Explore different ways of linking all the moves you know - there are endless combinations for you to find. Spinning with someone else can also help, as you feed each other inspiration and trick ideas. You will often see something being done that you didn't realize was possible or perhaps new moves that you didn't realise existed.

You could also try a new discipline or circus skill toy like Poi. These work in many similar ways and are a lot of fun to play with. People who learn staff then poi find their staff spinning improves naturally while learning poi and vice versa. While it may not have occurred to you, Poi and Staff are both based on the same physical principles.

Sometimes it's not a new trick you're looking for, but a new style. There is a whole set of concepts I have mentioned in this book to get you started. Contact spinning and throwing styles are two types that I have mentioned, but there are many more. How about mixing gymnastics and staff spinning? My style, for example, is based far more on a martial arts style.

Appendix

Fire Staff Spinning

Fire spinning is an amazingly hypnotic, powerful and highly impressive art form. You don't have to be a professional to enjoy the beauty and thrill of fire spinning, but you do have to understand that fire is dangerous. You should be sure that you have practiced enough first without fire. Please read this whole section very carefully if this is your first time, paying close attention to all the do's and don'ts!

Anatomy of Fire Staffs

This is the **wick,** the bit that burns. Obviously a bigger wick means a heavier staff, but the fire will be bigger and burn for longer. The wick is usually made of Kevlar, a super tough fabric that is able to be soaked with fuel but won't actually burn itself - the fuel is what burns, not the wick. Over time however, the wick will blacken, fray and eventually need replacing. It is really important to regularly check the screws holding the Kevlar to the staff are tight. If you find any loose screws, tighten or replace them immediately before an accident happens, especially when dealing with multi-wick headed staffs. See page 97 for staff decorations.

The **handle grip** is there to prevent the staff from slipping while spinning. A commonly used grip is found on tennis rackets but many other grips work well too. It will also help you feel where the centre of your staff is. It is important not to pick a handle that will soak up fuel and to keep it in good condition.

The **shaft** must be made of a fire proof / resistant material. (Metal is the most commonly used for fire staffs.) This can be customised to different lengths, weights and thicknesses. (See page 11).

Tip: Why not use a pair of old socks to put over the ends when you're finished burning / performing. This will keep the soot off everything while you travel with it.

Before Lighting Up

Fire spinning, twirling, eating and even breathing have become quite popular these days, even so, fire's more destructive side should always be respected and remembered. Keep in mind the consequences, if you have any doubts, I suggest a visit to the burn ward at your local hospital. When uncontrolled, it can be one of the most destructive forces in nature, but don't fear it, as it can be a most beautiful and enchanting servant if you play safe. Practice is so important here, you should feel really comfortable spinning the staff without fire before you decide to light up.

Always carefully consider the wind stability, direction and speed before you start, especially before spinning off excess fuel - don't let people stand too close downwind of you!

Should you have the misfortune of catching on fire remember **- STOP, DROP AND ROLL!**

Safety Comes First!

This book isn't big enough to detail every possible fire hazard when spinning fire. Always think carefully about the situation, use common sense to assess every possible hazard, that way you're prepared when a mistake happens.

* DO NOT lose your respect for the fire. It will hurt you and your audience if not treated correctly.

* DO NOT fire spin without the right safety equipment, clothing and trained people present.

* DO NOT play with fire under the influence of any drugs *including* and especially alcohol.

* DO NOT fire breathe without professional training - people have died painfully trying this.

Minors should always be supervised when dealing with fire. It is a dangerous activity. Do not twirl without adult supervision if you are under 18.

Insurance

Before you light up you must get public liability insurance to spin fire. Remember the day you decide to spin fire without insurance could be the day a terrible accident happens to someone or something, costing you millions or worse.

Always Check Your Equipment

Check your equipment every time you use it. The time you forget to check it will be the time something goes wrong! Check the hardware, make sure it is secure; check handles and trim any frayed wick or wire. Also, staffs that use screws to hold wick on need to be tightened regularly as the wick shrinks over time. If you're using a multi-section staff, you should really check the connections before spinning as these connections can fail.

Safety of Others

Check out the fire spinning area you intend to use for flammables, things of value or things that might get in the way. Look out for trees, buildings, cars, etc. Be aware of local fire bans, local regulations and get permits if required. Ensure your fuelling area is well marked, out of reach of your animals, children, audience and well away from your spinning area.

Always have a fire blanket and / or fire extinguisher ready and waiting near by and make sure you know how to use them properly. At the very least have a damp towel or blanket - this should NEVER be used to mop up fuel spills. Never spin alone - ALWAYS have a "spotter" / fire safety person who will watch you and be prepared to deal with any accident that may happen.

Your "spotter" / fire safety person should keep an eye on the fuelling station, making sure the audience is kept a safe distance away - 3 metres should be a minimum.

If somebody does catch fire, they need to STOP, DROP & ROLL, then, the spotter should firmly place / wrap the wet towel or blanket around the victim to suffocate the flame. Do not pat and flap the towel around, it must be kept firmly against the victim's body to work correctly. You should practice your safety drills before you light up.

Be aware of the wind direction. You don't want your audience getting covered in spin off fuel or be in danger.

Please note that a garden water hose is not considered adequate for fuel fires and should only be used if nothing else is available.

What to Wear

Wear close fitting clothing made of 100% natural fibre like cotton jeans. Synthetic materials like polyester and nylon will catch fire very quickly and can easily melt to your skin - DO NOT USE THEM. If you are unsure, check the label or do a small test on the clothing before you start. Remove all jewellery that might get in the way.

Remember to tie up long hair, wear a hat or dampen long hair, and always avoid using hairspray - it can give your hair a really effective coating of extra flammable fuel, so don't use it if you're intending to light up. (Glitter Spray and any other spray is normally very flammable too).

Also don't keep your lighter anywhere on your body while you're spinning as it could get hit and the lighter could explode; yes, it HAS happened.

It's hard for you to see if your back is on fire. Make sure your "Fire Safety Person" is ready with a fire blanket / towel and that you both know where your fire extinguisher and first aid are if needed.

If you get fuel on your clothes, change them before you light up as only a good machine wash will get the fuel out so that they are no longer flammable.

Fuelling Up

No matter what fuel you choose to use you should understand the properties of the fuel (e.g. get a copy of the Material Safety Data Sheets, M.S.D.S.) before you use it and act accordingly. Fuels are different all over the word and even have different names for the same thing in different countries. Any combustible fuel is dangerous

Beware that you're breathing the fumes / soot from your fire and the fuel is carcinogenic and often contains chemical "fillers" which are not very good for you.

A good first choice is Lamp oil, otherwise use a more refined Kerosene (also called liquid Paraffin). Usually a clearer looking liquid creates less smoke when burned. You can use poorer quality Kerosene or Citronella Lamp Oil but these can be very sooty and smoky. Any of these will burn fairly well and are quite safe.

Camp fuel / white gas is good for indoor performances. It is highly refined thus it is about half as smoky as lamp oil and has a much hotter whiter flame. It evaporates quickly which means shorter burn times and cleaner stage areas. If you have your fire equipment pre-dipped & waiting during a fire performance try plastic bagging them to slow down fuel evaporation.

Mixing 50% Lamp oil and 50% Paraffin / Kerosene is popular for outdoor fire spinning performances. It can also be very dangerous unless you know what you are doing! Lamp oil burns a bit cleaner and paraffin is smokier - mixed together you'll get a longer burn time and nice orange flames.

Fuels to Avoid:

Petrol (Gasoline), Paint thinner and drinking spirits are all extremely volatile and the vapours are highly explosive. Under NO circumstances should you use these fuels! Alcohols such as methylated spirits are poisonous and do not burn effectively enough for fire spinning. Again do NOT use petrol under any circumstances.

Fuel Areas / Stations & Environmental Fuel Management

A good fuel station should consist of:

Fire safety equipment. (See page 94 for more details)

A roped off area at least 3 metres from the audience with easy access for you. There should be enough room for you to dip your wicks and spin off, as well as two containers - the "Fuel Dipping Bucket" and the empty "Spin Off Bucket". Fuel dipping area should be set apart from any naked flame.

Large clean metal paint cans with a lid work best for the buckets if you can get them. I would not recommend using any type of plastic container. Always secure the lid after dipping and before you light up so that there is no risk of the fuel bucket catching fire. The spin off bucket or bottle (see below) will capture your excess fuel, which can be added back to the fuel bucket. This is much safer than splashing your surroundings and the audience with fuel.

Spin off Bucket / Bottle

Both lamp oil and paraffin tend to spray the spinning area with an oily residue which can become slippery and unsafe. To avoid this, spin off your dipped staff somewhere else or into another bottle before lighting. This works by placing your soaked wick in the can, holding the staff and the handle of the bucket together. Swing the staff and bucket in a few circles which should force the excess fuel out and into the bottle. Finally take out your staff and pour the excess fuel back in your dipping bucket. You're ready to spin! A long stem grill lighter is useful when lighting the staff. When you first start fire spinning move slowly and let your excess fuel on the staff burn off a bit so you that you don't spray the audience or yourself. *This will also help you stay standing.*

Advanced fire spinners may play with excess fuel (see Fire Staff Volcano move page 93), but I wouldn't suggest this until you are very comfortable with both fire spinning and fire safety.

Staff Extinguishing & Extending Fire Equipment Life

Your fire equipment will last much longer if you look after it. After the fire has fully extinguished, dip the wick into fuel to cool the wick down. To put your fire out, check wind direction before you blow from the bottom of the wick / flame to the top or if blowing twice doesn't do it, completely smother with a fire blanket or wet towel.

First Aid for Burns

Remember the saying... "If you play with fire you **WILL** get burned!" This doesn't have to be the case if you're careful but accidents do happen. If you have burned an area badly, (any burn that starts to blister) seek immediate medical assistance. If you have burned fabric or clothing and it's stuck to your skin do not try removing it yourself, go straight to hospital. With all burns, try to treat them as quickly as possible.

For the more insignificant burns, (burns that do not blister), hold the burnt area under gently running cool water for about ten minutes. Remove any jewellery and clothes from the affected area, unless it is stuck to the flesh. If it is a minor burn only, you can cover it with a sterile, non-stick dressing. Burns get infected quickly so keep the area clean until you have found medical help.

Tea tree oil, lavender and aloe vera are very good treatments for pain relief and healing minor burns. Pouring cold water over your burn can also help with the pain.
If you get fuel in your eyes, rinse with running cold water for 15 minutes then get medical attention immediately.
If you swallow some fuel, **do not** induce vomiting but seek medical attention immediately.
Do not apply lotions or moisturizers.
Do not prick blisters.
Do not overcool with ice.
Do not put towels or adhesive bandages directly on your burn.

Fire Staff Volcano Move (Excess fuel spin off trick)

a.k.a. **Flaring (Burn Off)**

This is a visually amazing trick which is great for when you have just dipped and lit up. Be careful when performing this as you are playing with a lot of excess fuel. The idea of this move is to spin the staff along its central axis, causing the excess fuel to spin out away from the staff and ignite into two giant balls of fire. Before doing this it is very important to be aware of your surroundings and the wind direction. The dangerous balls of fire will blow into you if you're facing the wind the wrong way, so check and check again! You usually do this move at the start of a burn when you have excess fuel in the wicks. It is critical to do this move with plenty of control.

The volcano trick might leave fuel residue on the area you are performing in.

| Start with the staff horizontally in front of you holding its centre at the base of your palm. | Use the open palm of your top hand to roll / push the staff up your hand and into the air, while pulling the bottom holding hand back down. | The best results are when you get a lot of spin on the staff as it goes up. | Get the top hand out of the way, while pushing up slightly with lower hand causing the staff to fly up just above your head. | The staff should stay horizontal all the way up and back again ready for a really easy catch. |

Fire Staff Spinning Equipment List

First Aid

☐   Instructions on how to deal with burns and general first aid.

☐   A pair of scissors - to cut bandages and clothes off if needed.

☐   A roll of non-adhesive, non-fluffy bandaging / gauze.

☐   Mixed sized band aids.

☐   Painkillers - also handy to have when you hit your head!

Non Medical Safety

☐   Public liability insurance - to pay for any accidents involving third parties.

☐   A flashlight - as you're spinning fire in the dark you will need one to find things and help see things in an emergency.

☐   Lots of water - to rehydrate yourself after spinning or to cool a burn.

☐   Safety person / spotter.

☐   Fire extinguishing equipment - clean wet towels, fire blankets and fire extinguishers are considered standard.

☐   A safe area to spin fire - away from anything flammable or valuable.

☐   Suitable clothing.

☐   Checked all fire spinning equipment is working and safe.

Non Safety

☐   Staff(s) and other fire equipment.

☐   Fuel in a container designed for fuel, labelled and properly sealed.

☐   A fuel bucket.

☐   A spin off bucket.

☐   A wind proof lighter.

Other Spinning Objects and Tools

Cane / Umbrella Manipulation / Spinning

The word "cane" has many names: canes, walking sticks, and umbrellas. Most variations / manipulations involving the cane relate to the different balance points or the curved handle of the cane. Aside from this, they can be treated in a very similar fashion to staff spinning, but you'll figure that out when you get there!

The curved handle on a cane can be used to great effect. The two primary uses of the handle are:

1) To throw and catch the stick using different extremities of your body.

2) To twirl the stick about any of your extremities.

Extremities such as arms, legs, elbows, feet and ankles make good twirling pivots, as well as catching / throwing points.

Canes can also be used for balancing other objects, such as hats or balls!

Canes are also used as a weapon, in different martial arts, including Hapkido, Taijiquan, Bando, Taekwondo, Kuk Sool, and Hwrang-do.

Devil Sticks

a.k.a. **Devil Stick, Devil-Stick, Rhythm Stick.**

This discipline is also a form of gyroscopic juggling (like staff spinning), that uses two hand sticks and one or more main spinning sticks or batons. This form has its completely own set of movements and tricks but uses many of the same balance and spinning skills as staff.

Poi

This form of spinning is slightly different to the others as it does not use a stick yet is still considered object manipulation. Poi are basically balls on the ends of ropes, held in each hand and swung in various circular patterns, comparable to club twirling. It uses exactly the same rule / laws of planes, directions and speeds as you do in staff spinning, especially when talking about double staff movement. Because of this, whatever you learn with poi will only ever improve what you already know in staff and vice versa.

There are some great books and videos out there, so go check them out.

Decorations and Effects

You can decorate your staff once you know how to use it and what you want to use it for.

Attaching ribbons, sheets of fabric, or reflective foil around the entire length of the staff gives the staff a very personal touch.

Attach glow sticks on the ends for an indoor friendly, black-light reactive, safer version of your fire staffs. They come in every colour and are easily attached using electrical tape or zip ties.

Ribbons or flags look and sound great on each end of your staff for daytime use and are good for following planes when you are learning. When attaching ribbons and flags remember to point them slightly inwards, (45 degree angle from the staff end) making sure they run along the circumference of the circle that the staff will make when spinning. Using ripstop nylon makes a good noise as it flies through the air. Other materials make different sounds, so experiment.

Wicks can be added to each end for flaming fire staffs. You can even add multiple wick ends to the staff to create a number of fire circles while it spins, as shown to the right.

Advanced, insured, professional fire spinners even attach different types of stage pyrotechnics to the ends of the staff to create large dangerous firework displays. (Not recommended unless you are fully trained and insured for this!!!)

Secrets of a Good Performance

OK, so by now you can spin quite well; time to do a show.

Here are some tried and tested ideas to help you put a show together!

Variety

Variety is the key to an exciting show. Without using different techniques, people may get bored with the show very quickly.

Speed and Space: Different speeds create different, unique looking moves. Use all of the space and area provided to give the audience the best views of the show at any one point. Remember to try different planes and different foot positions.

Big and Small Movements: Moving from small circles to big full body circles looks really nice when mixed with throws and other tricks.

Space and Movement: Every move you do should use different space to help generate speed and movement, so for variety mix them up and try out different combinations.

Starts and Stops: Starting and stopping at the right time can make your tricks more powerful and dramatic, especially if you are using music. These are also great opportunities to interact with the audience even if it is just a big smile.

Different Body Movements: Try putting your body in different and unusual positions to do a move you already know. For example, start off sitting on the ground doing a Rotor then figure out an interesting way to get onto your feet while transitioning to a different move. Flexible people have massive advantages here!

Dance: Don't forget to move with the timing and flow of the staff. Dance with the rhythms you make and feel the momentum as it moves you around.

Interacting with the Crowd

Face the right direction for the move you are doing. It is really important for you as the performer to be constantly thinking about what the audience is seeing and how to make that look good. Remember you can move your body without having to change foot direction (see page 31 for turns).

Smile - try to relax and show them you are enjoying yourself and they will relax and enjoy it with you. If you make a small mistake - CARRY ON and forget about it. Look worried and they will worry too. At the end, no matter how bad you might think you were, don't forget to pause for the applause and smile!

Know Your Music and Limitations

Practice, practice, practice!!!

Practice with the music you're going to use until you get it right. Don't perform tricks that you are still practicing unless you're really sure they look good. There is nothing worse then watching a really good show and seeing someone drop their equipment or make a really obvious mistake. There is a time and place to practice those hard moves. When you have put the time and practice in you should know that you will always pull it off with style and confidence. If you're not sure about it, save it for another day and enjoy the moves you are good at now.

Perform with Everything You Have

When you show emotion the crowd feels it. Come onto the stage full of energy and the audience will feel that and feed off it. The atmosphere is set by the impression you make the second you walk on stage - you have the power to make them love you, you just have to give a little in return.

Choreography

A choreographed show is very different to just spinning continuously, which is usually referred to as free-styling. It takes a lot of time, energy and patience to put together a good show, but is always worth it at the end when you have worked up a hugely enthusiastic audience. There are hundreds of ways of doing this, so this is only a rough guide to help you on your way. How long it should take will depend completely on you and the people you wish to choreograph together. Remember, you can only be as fast as the slowest person in the group.

Outline

First brainstorm as many thoughts, ideas and tricks down on paper as possible and make an outline of what you want to do and how you would like to display it. Figure out roughly what moves you want to start with, where it should build and how grand you wish to make the finish. You can also figure out here what to wear, what the stage area will look like and what music might work. Getting this clear picture on paper will help everyone see what you propose and will inspire more thoughts. Think of an overall mood, style, running theme or form.

Music

Now it is time to to think about whether you will have music and what it may be. When picking tunes think about a track that isn't too long or short and has a variety of rhythms and beats, for example a typical stage show is about 4 minutes or more. Often the burn time of the equipment you're using will also dictate how long you can spin any one tool. The music should help create an atmosphere and take you on a little journey. Unless you want to work with them specifically, lyrics should generally be avoided, as they detract from the performer who is spinning. Just remember it should be something that you enjoy moving to, as you're going to spend a lot of time listening to it!

Break-Down

Using your brainstorming work (which should have a list of moves you want to add) imagine how your moves will look at each part of your music and see what works best. Keep in mind that many moves look better from a certain viewpoint and can look bad if shown from the 'wrong' side.

It is helpful to write out a breakdown of the music, (e.g. 4 bars of 8 = slow build up section; 8 bars of 8 = faster, bouncy etc). Then try to plan out moves or movement style that works best for each part. This will also be a good reference later to help remind you what moves went with what exact piece of the song. There are often cues in the music to start or end a piece - try to respond to these in your choreography. Match the tempo / rhythm of your moves to the music as well as possible, so that if it slows down, speeds up or stops, so do you.

Try It

Now you have a list of moves, try them out to the music and see what you have. Often you might find that something doesn't work due to either speed, direction or plane problems. When this happens just try something else. There are endless possibilities so don't get hung up on forcing something to fit in the show. Also you can have non-scripted parts of your show where you might have someone do an amazing freestyle piece.

Fix It

Once you have it all put together the way you think it should be, run it through repeatedly. You will probably find places in it that either feel off or look wrong. Fix these issues and try again. It is worth getting a test audience to give you their opinions. Another good way of seeing what it looks like is to video it from the angle of the audience and use that as a reference to fix or change things. I have never seen a show work the first time, so keep trying and fixing.

Perfect and Repeat

This is such an obviously important part that so many people don't do properly. The choreography won't get good by itself especially when there are more than two people learning it. Spend as much time as needed to make everyone and everything look sharp and slick. Focus on small things such as hand position, footwork, etc and don't forget to smile! Once you are moving as one and everything is working you'll know it!

Group Choreography

Using the same techniques used to build choreography, dazzling shows can be created with groups of spinners and twirlers. Using different "formations" (ways of arranging yourselves on stage) and moves by performers that compliment each other, amazing sequences of performance can be achieved.

It might help to choreograph the show to a specific idea, theme, or story you would like to tell. Building the show up to a climax is a great way of making sure you pull out all the big tricks right at the end for the audience to go crazy for.

There are so many different types of formations to think about, but it will always depend on how many people you have spinning. Keeping things symmetrical is a sure way of knowing it will work. If there are odd numbers in the group try arranging them so that every member in the audience has a good view of something. Having spinners spin in a line across the stage is another all time favourite for a great front angle move. Be careful not to obscure each other from the audience. (Unless of course that's what you're trying to do).

Having everyone spin moves in complete unity is an awesome effect for the audience as long as the work has been put in and everyone is doing the exactly the same thing at the exact same time. It only takes one person making the slightest mistake for this to look really bad.

Index

Other Titles From Butterfingers Books

Poi Spinning

Michal Kahn

ISBN10: 1 898591 19 9

ISBN13: 9781898591191

The definitive contemporary guide to the ancient art.

The Encyclopaedia of Ball Juggling

Charlie Dancey

ISBN10: 1 898591 13 X

ISBN13: 9781898591139

Still the most comprehensive and entertaining book on the subject.

The Compendium of Club Juggling

Charlie Dancey

ISBN10: 1 898591 14 8

ISBN13: 9781898591146

Companion to the Encyclopaedia in the same easy style.

How to Ride Your Unicycle

Charlie Dancey

ISBN10: 1 898591 18 0

ISBN13: 9781898591184

A beginner's guide to the most ridiculous form of transport ever invented.

Contact Juggling

James Ernest

ISBN10: 1 898591 15 6

ISBN13: 9781898591153

The classic manual for this unique and graceful style.

Splitting the Atom and Other Yo-Yo Stuff

Richie Windsor

ISBN10: 1 898591 16 4

ISBN13: 9781898591160

The essential guide for anyone who owns a Yo-Yo Over half a million copies sold worldwide!

Notes

Notes

About the Author

Born in the UK, Johnathan Reynolds began his lifelong love affair with staffs from the age of 4, when his Grandfather began to teach him martial arts. At the age of 14, he realised while watching a fire staff spinner on Brighton beach, that he had found his new obsession. Transferring his martial arts staff skills from self-defence to fire staff spinning was so natural for him, it wasn't long before he found other like-minded spinners and learned everything he could.

By 18, Johnathan was performing professionally around the world. He now has a large collection of skills he uses in his acts which include poi spinning, stilt walking, club swinging, stage fighting, pyro-technics, costume design, as well as holding a Computer Science Degree with Honours.

Johnathan and his wonderful wife Helen are currently directing and performing in their own entertainments and events company called "Flaming Fun".